God Loves

Katrina J. Donald

(Name)

and so does

Kerse Church Creche

(Giver)

who gave this book on

30th October 2005

(Date)

God Loves Me Bible

BY
Susan Elizabeth Beck
ILLUSTRATIONS BY
Gloria Oostema

**CANDLE
BOOKS**

GOD LOVES ME BIBLE
Copyright © 1993 by The Zondervan
Corporation

Published in the UK by Candle Books 1995
Reprinted 1996, 1999, 2000, 2001

Distributed by STL,
PO Box 300,
Carlisle CA3 0QS

Enquiries from publishers should be
addressed to:
Angus Hudson Ltd,
Concorde House, Grenville Place,
Mill Hill, London NW7 3SA, England.
Telephone: +44 20 8959 3668
Fax: +44 20 8959 3678
ISBN 1-85985-049-9

Note to parents
*Whenever you read this book to your
child, you can encourage him or her to
participate. The repetitive phrase "God
loves me" was written so that, at your
prompting, your child can repeat the entire
phrase or simply the word "me."*

Printed in Singapore

The
Beginning

Creation

**In the beginning there was nothing.
Then God made the sky and the earth.**

Genesis 1

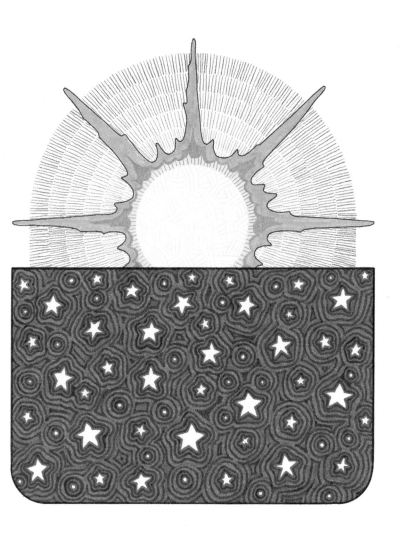

God made the sun and the stars.

God made the water.
God made the land.
He made the fish and the birds
and all the animals.
He put them on the earth.

Genesis 1

God loved his world.

Adam and Eve

God made two people to take
care of his world.
He made a man named Adam.
He made a woman named Eve.
Adam and Eve lived in a beautiful place
called the Garden of Eden.

Genesis 2

God loved Adam and Eve.

N oah

Noah was God's friend.
He listened to God.
God told Noah to build a big boat.
Noah put his family in the boat.
He put many animals in it too.
When a terrible flood came,
Noah and his family and the animals
were safe inside the boat.

Genesis 6–8

God loved Noah and his family.

Abraham

God chose Abraham to be the father
of a special nation of people.
God promised to give Abraham
plenty of land.
God promised Abraham as many
children as there are stars in the sky.

Genesis 12; 15

God loved Abraham.

Sarah

Sarah was very, very old.
God told her she would have a baby.
Sarah laughed.
An old lady couldn't have a baby!
But God gave Sarah and Abraham
a son. She named him Isaac.

Genesis 18; 21

God loved Sarah.

Isaac

Abraham had just one son – Isaac.
God asked Abraham to sacrifice Isaac.
Abraham was ready to obey God.
But God saved Isaac.
He stopped Abraham
from killing Isaac.
God promised to make Abraham
and Isaac famous and powerful
because they obeyed him.

God loved Isaac.

Rebekah

Rebekah was a very beautiful girl.
She was very special.
She was very brave.
Rebekah left her family
and moved far away.
She married Isaac,
and Isaac loved her.
Rebekah became the mother
of twin boys: Jacob and Esau.

Genesis 24–25

God loved Rebekah.

Jacob

Jacob had a dream.
He saw a stairway going up to heaven.
Angels walked up and down
the stairway.
And God stood at the very top.
God spoke to Jacob.
He promised to give Jacob
a lot of land and many children.
God promised never to leave Jacob.

Genesis 28

God loved Jacob.

 **R**achel

Rachel was a beautiful girl.
She took care of her father's sheep.
She married Jacob,
and he loved her.
Rachel had two sons:
Joseph and Benjamin.

Genesis 29–30; 35

God loved Rachel.

Joseph

Joseph was a special boy.
He had a very colourful coat.
He had very exciting dreams.
But Joseph's brothers didn't like him.
They sent Joseph far from home.
But God kept Joseph safe.
He made Joseph
a great man in Egypt.

Genesis 37

God loved Joseph.

God loved Noah, Abraham, Joseph
and all the people he had created.

And God loves me!

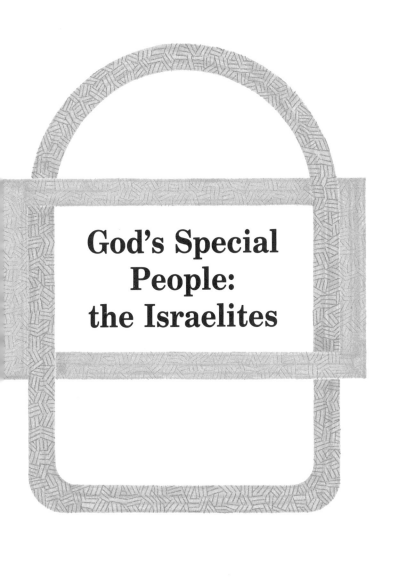

God's Special People:
the Israelites

The Baby Moses

Moses was a strong, beautiful baby.
His mother hid him from the soldiers
who were killing
the Hebrew baby boys.
She put baby Moses in a basket
and placed it in the Nile River.
A princess found Moses in the basket.
She kept him safe from the soldiers.

Exodus

God loved baby Moses.

The Leader Moses

Moses talked with God.
He did whatever God told him to do.
God spoke to Moses
from a burning bush.
God told Moses to help
his people the Israelites.
Moses became a great leader
of God's people.

Exodus

God loved the leader Moses.

The Israelite Slaves

God's special people lived in Egypt.
They worked very hard for the king.
They were unhappy,
so they prayed to God.
God sent Moses to ask the king
to let the people leave Egypt.
But the king said, "No!"
Then God sent ten terrible plagues –
frogs and grasshoppers
and boils and flies.
Then the king let God's
people leave Egypt.

Exodus 1:7–1

God loved the Israelite slaves.

Miriam

Miriam was Moses' sister.
She left Egypt with God's people.
She saw how God divided the Red Sea.
The water made two walls,
and Miriam walked across
the sea on dry ground.
When Miriam reached the other shore,
she danced and sang
a special song of thanks to God.

Exodus 14–1

God loved Miriam.

The Hungry Israelites

The Israelites took a long
trip in the desert.
They needed something to eat.
They were very hungry.
God sent a special bread from heaven
every morning to cover the ground.
The people called the bread manna.
They were never hungry again.

God loved his people the Israelites.

Moses

Moses led the Israelites
to Mount Sinai.
He climbed the mountain
to talk to God. Moses was on the
mountain for a long time.
God gave Moses ten rules
for the people to obey.
Moses called these rules
the Ten Commandments.

God loved Moses.

Caleb and Joshua

Twelve men went to explore
the promised land of Canaan.
Ten of the men were scared and said
the Israelites should not go there.
But Caleb and Joshua thought
the land was wonderful.
They knew that God would help
the people conquer Canaan.

God loved Caleb and Joshua.

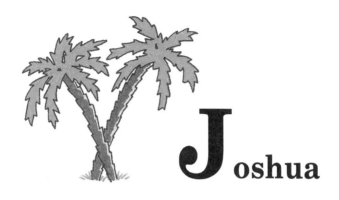

Joshua

Joshua was a great leader
of the Israelites.
He led God's people
to the promised land.
Joshua's army conquered
the city of Jericho.
They marched around the city.
They shouted and blew trumpets,
and God made the walls
of Jericho fall down.

God loved Joshua.

God loved Moses and Caleb
and Joshua and his special people,
the Israelites.

And God loves me!

God's People
in the
Promised Land

Deborah

Deborah was a leader of God's people.
When an enemy came to attack Israel,
Deborah led the army into a battle.
Deborah trusted God.
And the Israelites won!
Deborah wrote a beautiful
song of thanks to God.

God loved Deborah.

# The Weak Gideon

Gideon was weak. Gideon was small.
God wanted Gideon
to be a great leader.
But Gideon did not believe that God
could make him a great leader.
So he made God take a test.
Finally, Gideon believed he could do
what God wanted him to do.
With God's help Gideon
became a great leader.

48

God loved Gideon.

The Brave Gideon

Gideon was the leader of a huge army.
God told Gideon to make his army
smaller and smaller.
Gideon obeyed God.
Finally Gideon went to battle
with only 300 men.
With trumpets and empty jars
and God's power, Gideon's little army
scared the enemy away!

Judges

God loved Gideon.

Samson

Samson was strong.
Samson was special.
When Samson was young
he obeyed God.
But when he grew up,
he did not always obey God.
But God still used Samson
as a leader of the Israelites.

God loved Samson.

Ruth

Ruth was sad. Her husband had died.
She had no children, but she loved
her husband's mother, Naomi.
Ruth promised never to leave Naomi.
She promised to love
Naomi's God and Naomi's people.
God blessed Ruth.
He gave her a new husband and a son.

God loved Ruth.

Hannah

Hannah wanted a baby very much.
She went to the temple and prayed.
Hannah asked God to give her a baby.
God answered Hannah's prayer.
He gave her a baby boy.
Hannah named her baby Samuel.
Hannah loved Samuel,
and she sang a beautiful song
of praise to God for him.

1 Samuel 1–2

God loved Hannah.

Samuel

When Samuel was a little boy,
he lived in the temple.
One night he heard a voice
calling his name – once, twice,
then three times.
When the voice called again,
Samuel said, "Here I am, Lord."
Samuel listened to God.
He obeyed God all of his life.

God loved Samuel.

God loved Deborah and Samson
and Ruth and all the people
in the promised land.

And God loves me!

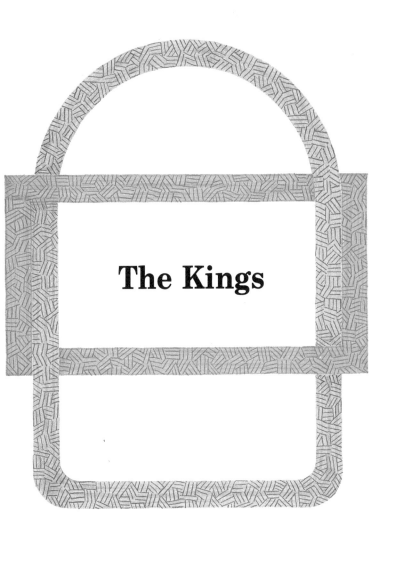

The Kings

Saul

Saul was taller than
the other men in Israel.
But Saul was shy.
He hid in the luggage when
the people wanted to make him king.
But the people found him.
They put a crown on his head,
and they made Saul
the first king of Israel.

God loved Saul.

The Shepherd Boy David

David was a shepherd boy.
He took good care
of his father's sheep.
He was strong and brave.
When a lion and a bear attacked
the sheep, David saved the sheep
and killed the wild animals.

God loved the shepherd boy David.

The Fighter David

David was too young to join the army.
But one day he fought the enemy
all alone!
He fought a giant named Goliath.
David was much smaller than Goliath,
and Goliath called him names.
But David trusted God, and he won!

God loved David.

King David

David was the youngest boy
in his family.
No one thought he could be a king.
But God chose David to be a great
and powerful king of his people.

1 Samuel 1

God loved King David.

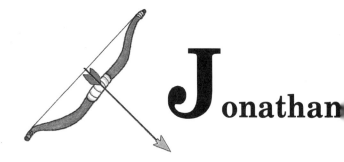 **J**onathan

Jonathan was the son of King Saul.
Jonathan was best friends with David.
He shot arrows
with David in the fields.
Jonathan protected David
when King Saul was angry.
Jonathan loved his friend David.

God loved Jonathan.

Abigail

Abigail was married to Nabal.
Nabal was a rich man,
but he was mean.
Nabal would not give food
to David and his men.
David was very angry.
But Abigail was smart and very wise.
She quickly brought bread and wine,
meat and fruit to David and his men.
She asked David
to forgive her husband.

1 Samuel 25

God loved Abigail.

 **S**olomon

Solomon was a good king of Israel.
He asked God to make him wise.
God made Solomon very wise.
God also made Solomon very rich.
Solomon built a beautiful temple
for God in Jerusalem.

God loved Solomon.

The Wise Solomon

Two women each had a baby.
But one baby died.
The mothers fought
over the living baby.
Solomon ordered the living baby
to be cut in half,
one-half for each mother.
One of the mothers cried,
"No, let the baby live!"
Then Solomon knew
she was the real mother.
And he gave her the baby.
Solomon was very wise.

God loved Solomon.

Joash

Joash was the king of Judah.
He wanted to make God's temple
a beautiful place again.
The people gave Joash a lot
of money to pay for the work.
Joash gave the money to the workers
who repaired God's temple.
Joash was a good king.

God loved Joash.

Hezekiah

Hezekiah was a good king of Judah.
He loved God very much.
Hezekiah got sick
and was about to die.
But Hezekiah didn't want to die.
He prayed to God.
God answered his prayer.
God let Hezekiah live 15 more years.

God loved Hezekiah.

Josiah

Josiah was a little boy
when he became king of Israel.
He was only eight years old!
One day the priests found
some very old books in the temple.
Josiah told the priests to read
the books to the people.
All the people loved to hear
what God said in the books.

God loved Josiah.

God loved David and Solomon
and all the kings of his nation.

And God loves me!

The
Prophets

The Prophet Elijah

Elijah loved God and obeyed him.
When there was no food to eat,
God sent birds to take care of Elijah.
The birds brought Elijah bread
and meat to eat
every morning and every night.

God loved the prophet Elijah.

Elijah

One day Elijah took a walk
with his friend Elisha.
Suddenly a chariot and horses
of fire flew between Elijah and Elisha.
Then a whirlwind came and picked
Elijah up and carried him to heaven.

God loved Elijah.

Elisha

Elisha had a good friend, a young boy.
One day the little boy died.
Elisha went to the boy's room.
He prayed to God.
Then Elisha lay on top of the boy.
Suddenly the boy sneezed seven times
and opened his eyes.
The little boy was alive again!
Elisha sent him back to his mother.

God loved Elisha.

Isaiah

God needed someone to bring news
to his people the Israelites.
One day God appeared to Isaiah.
He asked Isaiah to be his messenger.
At first Isaiah was afraid.
He didn't think he could do the job.
But then he said,
"Here am I. Send me."
Isaiah became a great messenger
of God to the Israelites.

God loved Isaiah.

Jeremiah

Jeremiah was a messenger of God.
He told the people bad news.
They didn't like what Jeremiah
told them so they put him
into an empty well.
Jeremiah sank deep in the mud.
After a little while, Jeremiah's friend
pulled him out of the well.
Now the people were ready
to listen to Jeremiah's news.
And everything he said came true.

God loved Jeremiah.

Jonah

God told Jonah to go to Nineveh.
But Jonah didn't listen.
He ran away from God instead.
He got on a ship and sailed away.
When a storm came,
Jonah was thrown into the sea.
A big fish swallowed Jonah,
but he didn't die.
Jonah prayed to God,
and God saved him.

God loved Jonah.

God loved Elijah and Isaiah
and Jonah and all his messengers.

And God loves me!

God's People Away From Home

Shadrach, Meshach, Abednego

Shadrach, Meshach and Abednego
lived in a country called Babylon.
The king wanted them
to worship a golden idol.
But the three men loved God.
They would not worship the idol.
So the king threw them
into a burning fire.
The flames were very, very hot.
But the three men did not get burned.
They came out of the fire safely.

Daniel

God love Shadrach, Meshach
and Abednego.

Daniel

Every day Daniel prayed to God.
One day the king said,
"No one may pray to God."
But Daniel prayed anyway.
The king ordered the soldiers to throw
Daniel into a den of lions.
But God kept Daniel safe.
The lions did not hurt him.
Daniel trusted God and obeyed him.

God loved Daniel.

 **E**sther

Esther became queen
of a great nation.
A wicked man made a plan
to kill all of the Israelites.
When Esther found out about the
plan, she told the king.
Esther trusted God,
and God's people were saved.

Esther 2–

God loved Esther.

Ezra

Ezra lived in Babylon.
He was a teacher.
He studied God's rules.
One day the king told him
he could go back home to Israel.
Ezra led many, many people
back to the city of Jerusalem.
With the help of the people,
Ezra rebuilt God's temple.

God loved Ezra.

Nehemiah

Nehemiah worked for
the king in Babylon.
One day the king told Nehemiah
he could go back home to Israel.
Nehemiah returned to Jerusalem.
He rebuilt the walls around the city.
Nehemiah trusted God and helped
the Israelites stay safe
from their enemies.

God loved Nehemiah.

God loved Daniel and Esther
and Ezra and all his people
who were far away from home.

And God loves me!

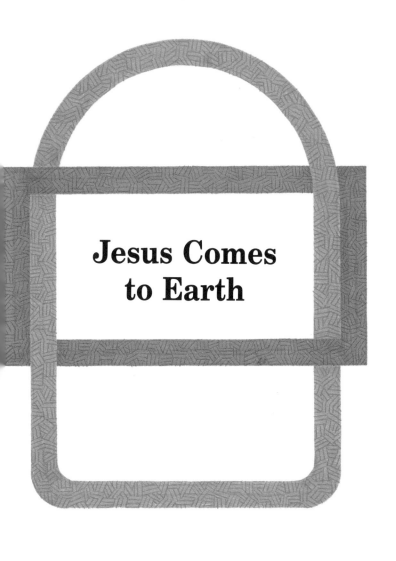

Jesus Comes
to Earth

Mary

Mary was a young girl who loved God.
One day an angel came to Mary.
The angel told Mary that
she would have a baby boy.
The baby would be God's Son,
and his name would be Jesus.
Mary was a wonderful mother
for Jesus.

Luke

God loved Mary.

Joseph

Joseph was a carpenter.
He loved Mary very much,
and he planned to marry her.
An angel told Joseph that Mary
was going to have a baby – God's Son.
Joseph believed the angel
and trusted God.
Joseph took good care
of Mary and the baby Jesus.

God loved Joseph.

The Baby Jesus

Jesus was a very special baby.
He was born in a stable in Bethlehem.
Angels appeared to the shepherds
and told them that Jesus was born.
A very special star
sparkled in the sky.
Magi followed the star from far away
to see Jesus and bring him gifts.
Jesus was the Son of God.

Matthew 2; Luke

God loved the baby Jesus.

The Boy Jesus

Jesus was 12 years old when he went
to Jerusalem with Mary and Joseph.
When it was time to go home,
Jesus stayed in the temple.
He listened to the teachers there
and asked many questions.
All the people were amazed
at how smart Jesus was.

Luke

God loved the boy Jesus.

John the Baptist

John the Baptist was a preacher.
He lived in the desert.
His clothes were made of camel hair,
and he ate locusts and honey.
John told the people that Jesus was
coming to save them from their sins.
John baptized many people
in the Jordan River.

Matthew :

God loved John the Baptist.

God's Son Jesus

Jesus came to John the Baptist
to be baptized in the Jordan River.
When Jesus came out of the river,
a dove landed on his shoulder.
A voice from heaven said,
"This is my Son. I love him."

God loved his Son Jesus.

# Mary and Martha

Mary and Martha were
friends of Jesus.
They let Jesus stay at their house.
They fed Jesus good food.
They listened to Jesus teach.
One day Martha got angry because
Mary listened to Jesus instead
of helping in the kitchen.
But Jesus told Martha that
Mary had chosen the right thing.

God loved Mary and Martha.

Zacchaeus

Zacchaeus was a very short man.
Zacchaeus wanted to see Jesus.
One day Zacchaeus climbed a tree
so he could see Jesus
when he walked past.
Jesus stopped to talk to Zacchaeus.
The Jesus had supper with him.

Luke 1

God loved Zacchaeus.

Lazarus

Lazarus was Jesus' friend.
He lived in the town of Bethany
with his sisters, Mary and Martha.
One day Lazarus got sick and died.
Jesus cried because
he missed his friend.
Then Jesus did something wonderful.
He made Lazarus come alive again!

John 1

God loved Lazarus.

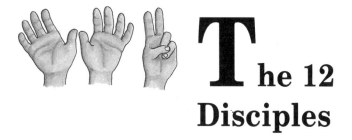

The 12 Disciples

Jesus had 12 special friends.
They were called his disciples.
The disciples were ordinary people.
But Jesus chose them to be
his closest friends
and to tell others about God.

God loved the 12 disciples.

A little girl

Jairus had a little daughter.
She was very sick.
Jairus went to Jesus for help.
Jesus came to Jairus's house.
Everyone was crying because
the little girl was dead.
Then Jesus did something wonderful!
He took the little girl by the hand
and made her alive again!

Luke

God loved the little girl.

The Little Children

Some people brought their
children to see Jesus.
They wanted Jesus to
touch them and to pray for them.
The little children were
very special to Jesus.
He talked to them
He gave them hugs!

God loved the little children.

The Risen Jesus

Jesus knew he had to die.
He knew God sent him to earth
to die for everyone's sins.
Many people didn't like Jesus.
They cheered when the rulers
chose to kill Jesus.
But Jesus did not stay dead.
He came out of his grave
in three days,
just like he said he would!

John 19–2

God loved his Son Jesus.

 **J**esus

For many days after Jesus died
and rose from the dead, he taught
his disciples many good things.
One day Jesus went up into heaven.
He disappeared behind a cloud.
His disciples were all alone.
Then two angels appeared.
They promised the disciples that
Jesus would come to earth again!

God loved his Son Jesus.

God loved Mary and Joseph
and Lazarus and all the people
Jesus knew on earth.

And God loves me!

God Loves
His World

Stephen

Stephen was very brave.
He told others about Jesus
even when it made them angry.
The people tried to stop Stephen
from talking about Jesus.
They threw stones and rocks at him.
Until Stephen died, he did not
stop talking about Jesus.

God loved Stephen.

Saul

Saul hated the Christians.
He had them put in prison.
One day a bright light
made Saul blind.
A voice told him to stop
hurting the Christians.
After a few days Saul could see again.
He became a Christian and
changed his name to Paul.
Paul told everyone about Jesus.

God loved Paul.

Paul

Paul was a great missionary.
He loved to tell others about Jesus.
He travelled a long way from home
to tell others about Jesus.
He wrote many letters that
are part of our Bible today.

God loved Paul.

Peter

Peter was in prison because
he was a Christian.
One night an angel came.
He told Peter to get up.
The chains fell off Peter's wrists.
Peter walked past the soldiers
and out of the prison.
Peter knew God's angel
had saved him.

Acts 12

God loved Peter.

God loves tall people.
God loves short people.

God loves all the people in his world.

God loves the people in my church.

**God loves the people
in my neighbourhood.**

God loves my mummy.

God loves my daddy.

And God loves me!

(Paste picture of child here.)

Yes! God loves _____!

God who made the earth,
The air, the sky, the sea,
Who gave the world its birth,
He cares for me.

God watches over me today,
While I sleep and while I play,
He lives in heaven up above,
And holds me in his arms of love.

GOD LOVES ME BIBLE
Index of Stories